WRITTEN BY SUSAN HARDESTY
ILLUSTRATED BY KRISTINA STEPHENSON & TERRY JULIEN

ISBN 0-7847-1805-9

12 11 10 09 08 07 06   9 8 7 6 5 4 3 2 1

Standard
PUBLISHING
Bringing The Word to Life™

Cincinnati, Ohio

The time had come to celebrate a great festival. A crowd of people started waving palm branches and laying them in the street. A very special guest was coming to the city to celebrate.

It was Jesus!

Where is Jesus?
What animal is Jesus riding into the city?
Do the people look happy or sad to see Jesus?
What color are the palm branches?

The first night of the festival, Jesus ate a great feast called the Passover. He ate the feast with twelve of his closest friends. Jesus warned his friends that something bad was about to happen to him. Then Jesus told his friends to remember that he would come back.

Can you count to twelve?
What are the friends eating?
Can you find a striped shirt?
Where is Jesus?

Some leaders of the people did not like Jesus. The leaders paid Jesus' friend Judas to help them arrest Jesus. The leaders had Jesus crucified even though he did nothing wrong. Jesus' friends were sad.

What are the leaders giving Judas?
How many crosses are on this page?

One man named Joseph was very sad because he loved Jesus. Joseph owned a cave called a tomb. Joseph and others who loved Jesus buried Jesus' body in the empty tomb. Then a big stone was rolled over to cover the doorway to the tomb.

Point to the big stone that covers the doorway.
What shape is the stone?
Where is Jesus?
What color is the jar that the woman is carrying?

The leaders who did not like Jesus were afraid because Jesus had said he would be back. The leaders ordered guards to stand watch at Jesus' tomb. The guards stood in front of the big stone that covered the tomb.

Where is the tomb?
How many soldiers are guarding the tomb?
What is covering the tomb?
Who is buried inside it?

Three days later some women went to visit Jesus' tomb early in the morning. A wonderful surprise was waiting for them there—the big stone was moved away from the entrance, and Jesus was not there!

He was alive!

What are the women holding?
Point to the tomb where Jesus
*   had been buried.*
Where is the stone now?
Where is Jesus?

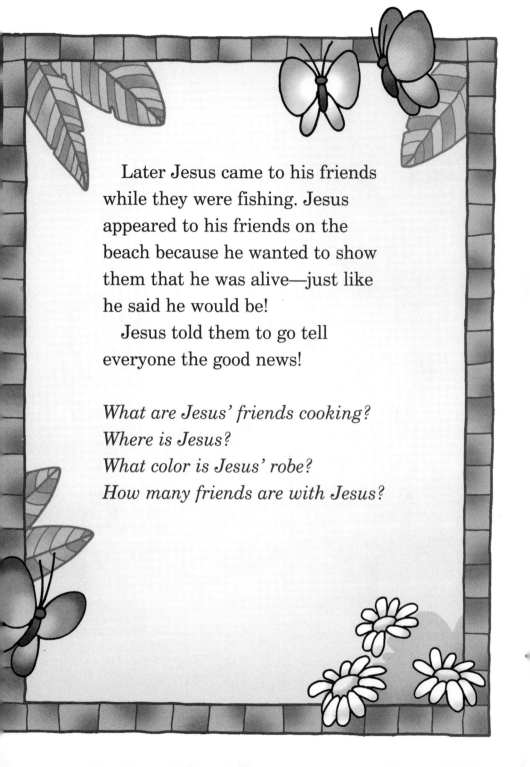

Later Jesus came to his friends while they were fishing. Jesus appeared to his friends on the beach because he wanted to show them that he was alive—just like he said he would be!

Jesus told them to go tell everyone the good news!

What are Jesus' friends cooking?
Where is Jesus?
What color is Jesus' robe?
How many friends are with Jesus?

Our friend Jesus is alive today! Jesus loves it when you talk to him. Jesus loves for you to tell others about him.

Go into all the world and preach
the Good News to everyone. —Mark 16:15